INSIDE

DRONES

BY KATE CONLEY

CONTENT CONSULTANT
John M. Robbins, PhD
UAS Program Coordinator
Embry-Riddle Aeronautical University

Core Library

An Imprint of Abdo Publishing
abdobooks.com

Cover image: A drone flies high in the sky to take pictures
of the ground below.

abdocorelibrary.com

Published by Abdo Publishing, a division of ABDO, PO Box 398166,
Minneapolis, Minnesota 55439. Copyright © 2019 by Abdo Consulting
Group, Inc. International copyrights reserved in all countries. No part of this
book may be reproduced in any form without written permission from the
publisher. Core Library™ is a trademark and logo of Abdo Publishing.

Printed in the United States of America, North Mankato, Minnesota
092018
012019

THIS BOOK CONTAINS
RECYCLED MATERIALS

Cover Photo: Shutterstock Images
Interior Photos: Shutterstock Images, 1, 12–13; Jay Janner/Austin American-Statesman/AP
Images, 4–5, 43; Steve Debenport/iStockphoto, 7; Marek Uliasz/iStockphoto, 10; iStockphoto,
14, 23 (satellite), 23 (background), 39; J. Galione/iStockphoto, 18, 45; Don Ryan/AP Images,
20–21; Nopparat Angchakan/Shutterstock Images, 25; Helen H. Richardson/The Denver Post/Getty
Images, 27; Ken Wolter/Shutterstock Images, 28; Imaginechina/AP Images, 30–31; J. M. Eddins Jr./
US Air Force, 33; Stephanie Aglietti/AFP/Getty Images, 34–35

Editor: Megan Ellis
Series Designer: Ryan Gale

Library of Congress Control Number: 2018949771

Publisher's Cataloging-in-Publication Data

Names: Conley, Kate, author.
Title: Inside drones / by Kate Conley.
Description: Minneapolis, Minnesota : Abdo Publishing, 2019 | Series: Inside
technology | Includes online resources and index.
Identifiers: ISBN 9781532117909 (lib. bdg.) | ISBN 9781641856157 (pbk) |
ISBN 9781532170768 (ebook)
Subjects: LCSH: Technological innovations--Juvenile literature. | Drone aircraft--
Juvenile literature. | Remotely piloted aircraft--Juvenile literature.
Classification: DDC 623.7469--dc23

CONTENTS

EYES IN THE SKY

On August 8, 2017, the Umpqua National Forest in Oregon had many dangerous storms. There were strong winds. By the end of the night, lightning strikes had started 15 forest fires. The forest had been dry before the storm. This meant that fighting the fires would be a challenge. But the crews had a new tool: drones. Drones gave crews a set of eyes in the sky.

Marcus Tobey was one of the trained drone pilots at the Umpqua fire. He operated a small quadcopter drone. It was outfitted with an infrared video camera. The camera

First responders use drones to help keep people safe.

helped Tobey see the fires at night. It sent real-time aerial footage to crews on the ground.

Tobey watched the fire. There were many small bits of burning wood in the air. Crews worried that they might start a new fire. On one flight, Tobey noticed something unusual. A new area glowed on the infrared camera. Tobey had discovered a new fire!

INFRARED CAMERAS

All objects give off infrared rays. They are a type of light ray. They cannot be seen without special equipment. Warm objects give off more infrared rays than cold objects. Infrared cameras detect these rays. They convert the rays into images. The color of the image is determined by its heat. Hot areas such as fires glow brightly. Infrared cameras on drones are a useful tool when it is hard to see. They can see a victim even in smoky, dark, or foggy conditions.

A NEW TOOL

Crews quickly put out the fire that Tobey spotted before it spread. This saved an estimated $50 million in damages. But it could not have happened without

People can build their own drones or purchase them at electronics stores.

Tobey and his drone. It was too dangerous for helicopters to fly over the area. Smoke had reduced the visibility to 100 feet (30 m). But the drone could fly where helicopters could not. It flew through the smoke. It gave real-time data that saved lives.

Drones like the one used in the Umpqua fire have become more common. Drones used to be expensive. But new technology has made drones cheaper in recent years. They are also easier to use. People can even buy drones at electronics stores. Drones come in many shapes and sizes. But they all have one thing in common. They are aircraft without pilots on board. They are controlled from other places, such as the ground. This is why drones are commonly called unmanned aerial systems (UASs).

LIVING WITH NEW TECH

The Federal Aviation Administration (FAA) sets the rules for US airspace. Drone pilots must follow FAA rules. These rules are different for personal drones and commercial drones, which are used in shipping and manufacturing. By 2020, the FAA estimates that as many as 7 million drones will be sold each year. But not everyone likes the idea of more drones taking to the skies. Some people worry that drones may invade their privacy. They believe that drones will take photos or videos without their permission. They also think drones might crash into things and become unsafe.

However, drones have the potential to be the next major tech revolution. They use a range of technology. Radio waves join with cutting-edge flight controllers, sensors, and the Global Positioning System (GPS) to create powerful vehicles. Many of today's drones are small and portable. Pilots can have

FAA REGULATIONS

In 2016, the FAA made rules for small Unmanned Aerial Systems (sUASs). They want to ensure people's safety and privacy. Drones must always remain in the visual line of sight (VLOS) of the pilot. Generally, drones may only fly at an altitude of 400 feet (122 m) or less. Drones cannot exceed 55 pounds (25 kg). Additionally, commercial drones may only be flown by a person with an FAA-issued remote pilot certificate.

Drones are easy to assemble and repair even for new users.

them flying in a few minutes. They can go places that are too dangerous for humans. They can use cameras in thick smoke. As the technology continues to improve, drones will change the way people live, work, and play.

STRAIGHT TO THE
SOURCE

In 2016, a team of 125 first responders in Europe took part in a study about drones. Their findings helped show how useful drones can be for first responders around the globe. Leo Murray is a first responder in Donegal, Ireland. He stated:

> When Search and Rescue (SAR) teams respond to a request for help, they do so in the face of ever changing challenges that can have a direct impact on the success of a SAR mission. . . . [The] use of a drone can help relay [information] to those responsible for coordinating the rescue, so that life changing decisions can be made quicker. Their use also helps to [reduce the] risk that team members have to face when responding, as well as saving on time to get to . . . locations.

Source: "The Use of Remotely Piloted Aircraft Systems (RPAS) by the Emergency Services." *EENA/DJI.* EENA, February 11, 2016. Web. Accessed August 9, 2018.

Changing Minds

Some people do not like how technology has overtaken modern life. Imagine you must convince these people about the benefits of drones. What evidence in the paragraph could you use to support your position?

DRONE BASICS

Remote-control (RC) aircraft have been in the skies since 1937. Ross Hull and Clinton DeSoto were hobby radio operators. They built an RC glider. It was the first demonstration of a remote-controlled flight. An interest in RC model planes grew. But early RC equipment was heavy. This limited what the aircraft could do. RC technology was later used to develop the first drones. Over time, drone hardware became lighter. Drones could fly high. They could travel far. This led to a renewed interest in drones.

AIRFRAMES AND PROPELLERS

Every drone has an airframe. It is the body of the drone. Other pieces of hardware attach to

Remote controls help pilots fly their drones. They can tell the drones which way to fly.

PARTS OF A DRONE

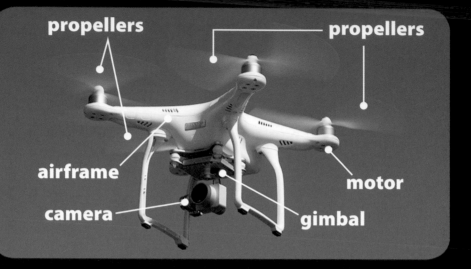

Quadcopters have four propellers. These propellers help the drone move. Look at the diagram above. What would be different if the drone only had one propeller? How would that affect its flight?

the airframe. Airframes can be made of plastic, wood, or metal. Some airframes are complex. They have many moving parts. Other airframes are simple.

Propellers attach to the airframe. They allow drones to fly. Some drones have four propellers. These drones are called quadcopters. The propellers look like fan blades. As they spin, propellers can provide lift. Lift is a force that pushes upward. It keeps a drone in the air.

A drone with a lot of lift can carry a greater payload. A payload could include a camera and other equipment.

The propellers on a drone do not all spin in the same direction. In a quadcopter, two propellers spin inward. The other two spin outward. This keeps a drone stable. It also allows it to take off and land almost anywhere.

Some drones have two long, fixed wings. This kind of drone looks similar to an airplane. It can use propellers or turbine engines, which are the same engines used in airplanes. It can carry heavy payloads. This is useful for making deliveries or carrying heavy equipment. However, most large fixed-wing drones need runways for takeoff.

MILITARY DRONES

The military uses drones both in the United States and in other countries. The first drone was used during World War II (1939–1945). It was called the Radioplane OQ-2. It was used as a target for US Army Air Corps gunners.

MOTORS AND BATTERIES

Each propeller on a quadcopter has its own small motor. Most new drones use brushless motors. They use magnets and electricity to power the drone. They are more reliable than older motors, which could catch fire. Each motor also has its own electronic speed controller. This determines the motor's speed and direction. It receives signals from a computer inside the drone.

A brushless motor gets its power from a lithium polymer, or LiPo, battery. These batteries are small and light. They also recharge. If charged correctly, one battery can be used again and again.

Some drones do not use LiPo batteries. They have gas-powered motors. These drones can fly for longer periods. They are heavier than drones with batteries. But this keeps them more stable in the wind.

CAMERAS

A drone's camera is useful. It is attached to the airframe on a gimbal. A gimbal is a support that pivots.

The gimbal keeps the camera horizontal, even if the drone dips or turns. This stabilizes the camera. It allows for smooth videos and sharp photos. A pilot can also move the camera using the gimbal. The camera can then capture different angles and viewpoints.

A drone's camera can be put to many uses. Filmmakers can take video with drones. Before, they had to use helicopters for aerial shots. But drones are cheaper, easier, and safer to use. Some cameras on drones can map the land. They can find people who are lost. They can also

TV SHOW DRONES

Some TV shows use drone cameras to capture footage. *Game of Thrones* films some scenes in Iceland. During filming, temperatures got down to -4 degrees Fahrenheit (-20°C). The winds were strong. It was hard for helicopters to fly.

The *Game of Thrones* production team used drones to get the shots they needed. The drones could fly closer than traditional helicopters. They could also fly at a moment's notice.

FPV cameras help pilots see where the drone is flying.

be used to inspect power lines, monitor crowds, and even save lives.

The cameras provide a first-person view (FPV). This allows pilots to see what the drone cameras see. Pilots can then decide what to do with the data. FPV images are transmitted from the drones to smart devices.

In January 2018, two teenagers swam in the ocean off the coast of New South Wales, Australia. People noticed the teenagers struggling to swim. They notified a lifeguard. The ocean was very rough. There were 10-foot (3 m) waves. The lifeguard immediately launched a drone. It was called the Little Ripper. The lifeguard quickly located the swimmers with the camera on the drone. He dropped a flotation pod that the drone was carrying. The teenagers safely returned to shore. It took less than two minutes. It marked the first-ever rescue of its kind.

Today the military uses drones to perform tasks that are too dangerous or difficult for humans. They may fly over an area to identify targets. They may gather information for future missions. In some cases, drones carry and launch weapons such as missiles.

EXPLORE ONLINE

Cameras can change drones from toys to life-saving tools. But some people worry their privacy is being invaded by drones with cameras. They do not want to be filmed without their knowledge. Read the article at the site below. Do you share these privacy concerns? What are some possible solutions to the privacy problem?

HOW DRONES RAISED PRIVACY CONCERNS ACROSS CYBERSPACE
abdocorelibrary.com/inside-drones

CHAPTER
THREE

COMMUNICATING WITH DRONES

Hardware and software work together to communicate with the pilot and fly the drone. A flight controller is a small circuit board. It acts as the drone's brain. It has a microprocessor and sensors.

Sensors provide information to the microprocessor. They may monitor the drone's speed, position, or direction. A microprocessor is a part inside a computer that controls it. The microprocessor uses information from the sensors to adjust the drone's flight. For example, if a strong wind blows the drone, the microprocessor adjusts the flight controls.

Ground Control Stations monitor drone flights and controls. In this station in Arlington, Oregon, a pilot watches the drone on several computer monitors.

It may tilt the drone left or right. It may have the drone move up or down. This keeps the aircraft stable.

INERTIAL MEASUREMENT UNIT

Most flight controllers have a group of sensors. Together, the sensors are called the Inertial Measurement Unit (IMU). An IMU may include a magnetometer. This provides a compass reading. Accelerometers detect a drone's linear movements. This includes flying forward or backward. A pressure sensor calculates the drone's altitude. Some IMUs also contain a gyroscope. This detects rotational movements such as when the drone dips down or rolls to the side. These sensors can describe a drone's position and movement at any point in time.

Ground Control Stations (GCS) help pilots send signals to drones. Some GCS are small radio controllers. Others are very large. They need multiple people on the flight crew. They are in large buildings.

GCS programs run on computers. Using the software, the pilot can see through the drone camera. She can also steer the drone from the ground.

OPERATING A
DRONE

Drones send and receive a lot of data using GPS satellites. They also send and receive data through radio waves. A pilot can use this data to do many things. Look at the infographic below. How might the pilot use data from the drone's camera? What could the drone tell him about the environment?

A drone signal is received by a GPS satellite in space. The satellite then sends the drone information about its location.

A drone sends the GCS video data from its FPV camera. The pilot then uses the controller to tell the drone which way to fly.

A drone and its pilot communicate using receivers and transmitters. The transmitter is on the remote. When the pilot moves the remote's joystick, the transmitter sends out radio waves. The drone's receiver picks up the radio waves. It sends them to the flight controller. The flight controller converts the radio waves into signals the motors can understand.

Drones can transmit information back to the pilot, too. For example, a drone with a camera can send the images to its pilot. Smartphones and tablets can pick up the radio waves. This allows drones to transfer images and videos directly to a pilot's device.

APPS FOR DRONES

New apps allow pilots to fly their drones from smartphones and tablets. All of the flight controls are on the app. The drone and device connect using radio waves known as Bluetooth. The device and the drone use Bluetooth to find each other. Then they can communicate.

Some controllers for drones connect to the pilots' smartphones. Other drones are entirely flown by apps, so the smartphone is the only controller.

Apps can also make flying drones easier and more fun. Some apps provide data about each flight a drone takes. These apps allow pilots to keep logs of flight times, distances, and battery power. Other apps provide information on flight conditions. They provide pilots with wind speeds, visibility, and weather forecasts. These elements affect drone flights.

Apps also allow pilots to pre-program flight paths. This is useful for pilots who want to fly long or complex routes. It is also useful for pilots who want to take video. They can move the gimbal to get the best angles and views. They do not need to steer in real time.

Some drones also have a social element. They allow drone pilots to connect with each other. After opening the app, a pilot can see pins on a map. Each pin represents another drone user. The maps also point out good locations for flying drones in the area. These apps also allow users to share images they've taken with their drones.

Apps can help pilots follow the FAA rules.

WI-FI DRONES

Radio waves are a type of energy that flows through space. It allows for a wireless signal between two or more devices. Wi-Fi is a type of wave that drones commonly use. These waves are similar to radio waves. Many new drones come with an onboard Wi-Fi system. This means the drone produces its own Wi-Fi signal. It does not need to join any networks. Instead, pilots can connect their devices directly to the drone.

A sign outside an airport in Minneapolis, Minnesota, warns pilots about flying drones nearby.

For example, pilots need special permission to fly drones within controlled airspace around an airport. The FAA describes this as within five miles (8 km) of the airport. The pilot may not know an area well. He may not realize how close he is to an airport. The app alerts the pilot. It also provides a way to get permission from the FAA.

A drone can use its GPS unit to take photos of specific locations. The pilot can even plan the route before the flight.

GPS

Apps are just one source of information for drone pilots.

A GPS unit is also important. It receives information

from a network of satellites. GPS can relay the drone's

position to its pilot. The GPS data is very accurate. It can pinpoint a drone's position within just a few centimeters. This is useful if the drone accidentally leaves the pilot's line of vision.

Many new drones also have a return-to-home (RTH) feature that uses GPS. A pilot sets a home point. Once the point is set, a pilot just has to press a button on the remote. Then the drone uses GPS to return home. This can be useful in many ways. If a pilot loses site of the drone, he can press the RTH button. If the battery gets low, the drone will automatically return home. And, if the drone loses connection with the controller, it can return home.

FURTHER EVIDENCE

Chapter Three discussed apps that can help drone pilots. What is the key point of the chapter? The article at the link below discusses how archaeologists use drones to find ancient civilizations. Find a quote from the article that supports the chapter's main point.

HARVARD BUSINESS REVIEW: DRONES GO TO WORK
abdocorelibrary.com/inside-drones

THE FUTURE OF DRONES

In 2017, the FAA predicted the future of air traffic through the year 2037. It believes there will be many more drones. The number of hobby drones may even triple. In 2016, there were 1.1 million drones. The FAA predicts 3.5 million of them in 2021. Commercial drones are also on the rise. The FAA predicts that number will increase from 42,000 in 2016 to as many as 1.6 million in 2021. Many industries such as construction and mining are exploring future uses for drones.

As users become more familiar with the technology, they want their drones to be capable of more things. The drone industry

Deliveries are just one type of technology in the future of drones.

is racing to keep up with demands. Drone buyers want aircraft that can fly for long periods of time before needing electricity or fuel. And businesses experimenting with delivery drones want aircraft that can handle large payloads.

LINES OF SIGHT

The FAA states that drones must always be in the VLOS of the pilot. This is to keep people safe. But some pilots want to send their drones farther. They want the drones to go beyond visual line of sight (BVLOS).

Some military drones already use BVLOS. These drones communicate with the pilot using a satellite. But BVLOS can have many commercial and personal uses. These drones could deliver packages. They could also inspect dangerous areas that are farther away. In 2018, the FAA allowed the company Xcel Energy to fly drones BVLOS. They inspected power lines. The FAA may allow more BVLOS flights in the future.

The MQ-9 Reaper is a drone flown BVLOS by the US Air Force. Pilots fly it on combat missions.

CARGO

In December 2013, Amazon founder Jeff Bezos revealed his plans to deliver packages using drones. A drone could possibly deliver a package in 30 minutes. Amazon is not alone. Other large companies such as Walmart

Some delivery drones in Rwanda are launched from the ground. They deliver blood to 21 clinics in rural areas.

and Google want to use drone delivery systems. Drones may be the delivery system of the future.

The delivery process does not need a pilot. Instead, the drone uses GPS coordinates. A computer system

sends the drone the coordinates for the customer's address. It then flies there with no additional input. After it makes the delivery, the drone automatically returns to its warehouse. However, drone delivery systems would fly BVLOS. As of May 2018, drone deliveries are not possible in the United States. Some business leaders want to change these restrictions.

Delivery drones already appear in other parts of the world. In Rwanda, drones are being used to deliver life-saving medical supplies. Doctors in remote areas can text a company called Zipline with an order. Workers pack the requested medicines into a fixed-wing drone. Operators set its course using GPS. Then the drone flies to the delivery site and drops the supplies there.

POWER SOURCES

Most of today's drones get their power from batteries. But current LiPo batteries only provide a short flight time. Most small drones can fly for 10 to 30 minutes depending on the wind conditions and the payload. Researchers are working to find new power sources that allow for longer flights.

Solar-powered batteries are a possible solution. Solar cells are thin, light strips. They attach to the drone's airframe. They turn energy from the sun into a form that the drone's motors can use. Solar cells provide power without weighing down a drone like batteries do.

Solar-powered drones would automatically recharge as they fly. That means they could have very long flight times. Some researchers predict that solar-powered drones could fly for years at a time. A long flight time has many uses. Solar-powered drones could monitor changes in the environment such as melting glaciers. They could also transmit internet signals to people in hard-to-reach areas.

SOLAR CHARGERS

While solar-powered batteries are still in the testing phase, drones can harness solar power in other ways. A number of companies now sell solar-powered charging kits. The drone battery is connected to a small solar panel. Energy from the sun goes to the panel. It recharges the battery. This is especially useful for pilots who want to fly their drones in remote areas where electricity is hard to access.

AI DRONES ON SITE

Early versions of AI drone equipment are being tested by Komatsu, a Japanese construction firm. The AI drones are paired to construction equipment such as bulldozers. The drones provide operators with a 360-degree view around the equipment. This can help prevent accidents. When the job site changes, the AI drones provide operators with real-time directions and information.

ARTIFICIAL INTELLIGENCE

Artificial Intelligence (AI) is another type of technology that could affect how people use drones. AI is the ability of a computer to think like a human. When presented with a problem, AI is programmed to find a solution using reasoning. It also learns from its experiences. Then it applies that information to new situations.

The possibilities for drones equipped with AI are limitless. Drones working as security cameras could not only take footage but also call the police if needed.

Drones can take aerial photographs of electric power facilities. In the future, they may even be able to repair any problems they find.

This would reduce the need for security officers.
AI drones could also be used to inspect cell phone towers, powerlines, or wind turbines. They could then analyze the data and suggest repairs. They might even coordinate maintenance schedules and estimate costs. This would keep humans from performing the dangerous inspections. It would also provide more reliable data.

While AI and solar-powered drones are just in the early stages of development, the technology is improving quickly. Drones are becoming smarter and more efficient. The RC model airplanes from the 1930s have been transformed into cutting-edge vehicles.

New technology has made drones affordable and easy to use. This has led people to experiment with new ways that drones can do tasks. From inspecting power lines to keeping people safe, drones have the potential to change the way people approach business, defense, and fun.

STRAIGHT TO THE
SOURCE

A customer in England, placed an order through Amazon on December 7, 2016. A drone delivered the package 13 minutes later. It was the first package Amazon delivered by drone. Jeff Bezos, the founder of Amazon, spoke about the autonomous drone delivery trials:

> [The drone] lands by itself, it navigates by itself. You can fly more than 50 miles per hour, it has a 20-mile range roundtrip, and can deliver packages 5 pounds or less. It's going to work really well. . . . [You] just need a landing field, and if you have a landing field you can mark it with . . . a symbol you can print out on your printer and put it wherever you want the vehicle to land. . . . If [the drone] sees anything that makes it nervous, it can divert or phone home for help and get a human to help it land. It's really an extraordinary technology.

Source: Jeff Bezos. "Jeff Bezos Shares His Vision for Package Delivery." *GeekWire.* YouTube, October 23, 2016. Web. Accessed August 9, 2018.

Point of View

Bezos has been promoting a drone delivery service since 2013. FAA rules have prevented it from taking place in the United States. Should the FAA allow drone delivery? Are there any downsides to it?

FAST FACTS

- Drones are vehicles that operate without onboard pilots. Computers or pilots on the ground direct the drone's operations.

- The development of LiPo batteries and microprocessors made drones cheaper and easier to use.

- Drone technology advanced rapidly in the 2010s. People began putting drones to work in a variety of new jobs, such as aerial photography, product delivery, and land surveying.

- During natural disasters, drones can aid rescue workers by surveying damage. They can also deliver water and medicine to victims that rescue crews cannot reach.

- Using drones for high-risk work, such as inspecting power lines, reduces the number of dangerous situations a worker may have to face on the job.

- Drones can fly in conditions that would be too dangerous for piloted aircraft, such as low visibility or severe weather.

- The military uses large, high-power drones for special missions. They can survey enemy territory, identify targets, and drop weapons.

- Drones are popular among hobbyists. The FAA estimates the number of drone owners will triple between 2016 and 2021.

- One of the drawbacks of drones is their short battery life. Researchers are working on ways to improve this, such as by powering drones with solar cells.

STOP AND
THINK

Tell the Tale

Chapter Two discusses how Ross Hull and Clinton DeSoto created the first RC model airplanes. Imagine you are designing an RC airplane. Write a paragraph about the problems you encounter. What kinds of technology could help you solve these problems?

Say What?

Learning about drone technology involves lots of new words. Find five words in this book that you had never heard before. Look them up in a dictionary to find their meanings. Then write a paragraph that uses all five of the words correctly.

Take a Stand

Some people worry that the increase in drones will violate people's privacy. Do you agree or disagree with this viewpoint? Make a list of five reasons to support your opinion.

Why Do I Care?

You may not have any interest in flying your own drone. But that doesn't mean drones are not useful. Think of three ways a drone could make your life easier or safer. Write a paragraph about how a drone could help you in your daily life.

GLOSSARY

aerial
happening in the air or the atmosphere

brushless motor
a motor that is controlled by a computer and uses magnets to turn

circuit board
a thin board that contains the electrical circuits for a device such as a computer or smartphone

commercial
being involved in buying, selling, and trading

coordinates
a set of numbers used to find a precise location on a map

Global Positioning System (GPS)
a system of satellites in Earth's orbit that helps users determine location

infrared
light rays that any warm object emits

payload
the cargo a vehicle carries

visibility
the distance that can be seen with the naked eye

ONLINE RESOURCES

To learn more about drones, visit our free resource websites below.

Visit **abdocorelibrary.com** for free Common Core resources for teachers and students, including vetted activities, multimedia, and booklinks, for deeper subject comprehension.

Visit **abdobooklinks.com** for free additional online weblinks for further learning. These links are routinely monitored and updated to provide the most current information available.

LEARN MORE

Dougherty, Martin J. *Drones.* New York: Scholastic, 2014.

Yomtov, Neil. *War on Terror Technology.* Minneapolis, MN: Abdo, 2018.

INDEX

About the Author

Kate Conley has been writing nonfiction books for children for more than ten years. When she's not writing, Conley spends her time reading, drawing, and solving crossword puzzles. She lives in Minnesota with her husband and two children.